Mao Zedong

WITHDRAWN

LEADERS OF ASIA
General Editor: K.G. Tregonning

Field Marshal Plack Phibun Songkhram by B.J. Terwiel
Jinnah by K. McPherson
Sun Yat-sen by Richard Rigby
Jawaharlal Nehru of India 1889–1964 by Ian Copland
Tunku Abdul Rahman by A.M. Healy
Nakano Seigo by L.R. Oates
Ho Chi Minh by Milton Osborne
Jiang Jie-shi (Chiang Kai-shek) by J.S. Gregory
Zhu De (Chu Teh) by Shum Kui-kwong
Gandhi by Hugh Owen
Zhou Enlai by Merrilyn Fitzpatrick
Aung San by Aung San Suu Kyi

Mao Zedong

Paul Rule

Leaders of Asia Series

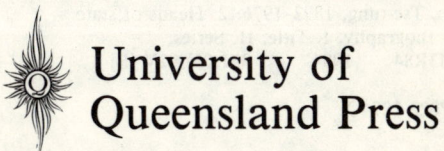
University of
Queensland Press

First published 1984 by University of Queensland Press
Box 42, St Lucia, Queensland, Australia

© Paul Rule 1984

This book is copyright. Apart from any fair dealing for the purposes of private study, research, criticism or review, as permitted under the Copyright Act, no part may be reproduced by any process without written permission. Enquiries should be made to the publisher.

Typeset by University of Queensland Press
Printed in Hong Kong by Warren Printing Co Limited

Distributed in UK, Europe, the Middle East, Africa, and the Caribbean by Prentice Hall International, International Book Distributors Ltd, 66 Wood Lane End, Hemel Hempstead, Herts., England

Distributed in the USA and Canada by Technical Impex Corporation, 5 South Union Street, Lawrence, Mass. 01843 USA

Cataloguing in Publication Data

National Library of Australia

Rule, Paul, 1937- .
   Mao Zedong.

   Includes index.

   1. Mao, Tse-tung, 1893-1976. 2. Heads of state — China — Biography. 3. China — Politics and government — 1949-1976. I. Title. (Series: Leaders of Asia).

951.05'092'4

Library of Congress

Rule, Paul, 1937- .
   Mao Zedong.

   (Leaders of Asia series, ISSN 0157-3268)
   Includes index

   1. Mao, Tse-tung, 1893-1976. 2. Heads of state — China — Biography. I. Title. II. Series.
   DS778.M3R84   1984   951.05'092'4 [B]   83-21673

ISBN 0 7022 1874 X

Introduction

This book is one of a series of monographs entitled Leaders of Asia. Each book is a brief but stimulating study of a man or woman who has contributed to the shape of Asia. Through a study of his career will emerge a greater knowledge of his country's place in the contemporary scene.

It is vital for Australians to understand the region of their future. It has been neglected in our studies for too long. This book, as part of a series, is aimed at enriching our awareness of the multicultural, turbulent, dynamic nations of Asia which are now impinging ever more steadily on our national consciousness.

As a biography this book can be read by itself with enjoyment. History is not merely the story of great men, but there is hardly a better way of studying it than by reading of them. If you knew little of the man or the country, your interest in both will be increased by this biography. The pleasure of a good tale makes understanding easy.

But as well, a monograph as part of a series is the ideal way to enrich a formal course of study. Gradually aspects of Asia are being offered to secondary and tertiary students in Australia in many ways. Our myopic concentration on Europe is diminishing, and not before time Asian studies are reaching the classroom and lecture theatre. Their textbooks need buttressing. Student interest needs sustaining. These brief biographies, complete with bibliographies, are intended to supplement those undergraduate and secondary school courses and to stimulate such studies.

Possibly as part of that stimulation the individual student will feel encouraged to dispute with the author, delve deeper into the subject, perhaps develop a language skill and visit the land being studied. By regarding Asia as foreign and unknowable, we risk the future of our country. By appreciating its culture and by understanding the contribution of its leaders, we help forge bonds that will enrich us all.

My aim as general editor of the series has been to bring forward young scholars who are helping to give Asian Studies a sound base in Australia. Here is Asia as seen by Australians. As a former Raffles Professor at the University of Singapore and now Headmaster of my old Australian school, I try and bridge the narrow gap between senior student and undergraduate. They share a level of intelligent interest with that of the general reader. This series is commended to them.

K.G. Tregonning
General Editor

Preface

This short life does not pretend to give a final evaluation of Mao Zedong.* Firstly, we are far too close to the man and his career to see him in true perspective, although, for what it is worth, the writer believes his direct influence will last much longer than many China watchers are now claiming. During the trial of the Gang of Four in late 1980, his wife, Jiang Qing (Chiang Ch'ing), attempted to associate Mao closely with her activities, and it is clear from the frequency of covert allusions to the "Gang of Five" that many Chinese believe him to be at least partly responsible for the excesses of the Cultural Revolution. But this does not amount to a repudiation of his achievements. China today is still too much Mao's China to be understood apart from the man.

This close identification of Mao Zedong with the central events of the history of China during his long life (1893-1976) makes the task of the biographer peculiarly difficult. One may attempt to disentangle the man from the myth, but the task is both impossible and probably misguided. It is impossible because there are few available contemporary documents relating to the crucial events of his career; revolutionaries in hiding and under attack do not keep records, and Communist bureaucracies do not open their more intimate archives to outsiders. But it may also be grossly misleading. Mao's impact on China was precisely through the myth, the public image of the "Great Teacher, Great Leader, Great Supreme Commander and Great Helmsman".

We do, of course, have memoirs and revelations by former colleagues and associates, some hostile some adulatory, but these are often contradictory and partial. We have Mao's official (and perhaps more useful, unofficial) collected works, but Stuart Schram and others have shown the extent to which the

---

*The Pinyin romanization of Chinese names is used throughout this monograph.

texts of Mao's writings have been doctored. We also have the impressions and records of conversations with Mao by Western visitors. The most important of these is undoubtedly the "autobiography" recounted over several evenings in 1936 to the American journalist Edgar Snow (see "Further Reading" at end of book). But Mao was well aware that he was speaking for the record and at a time when he was hoping for outside support in his bid for national power. Nevertheless, Mao's writings and talks give us many insights into his character and motivation.

Our major source for an understanding of Mao must be an analysis of his deeds. There are men, and Mao is clearly one, whose lives are so closely bound up with the times they lived in that it is nearly impossible to determine how much influence they had on events. Yet this very fact may indicate that Mao's genius mainly consisted in his reading his times aright.

This last point raises the question of "Maoism", of Mao's contribution to Marxist-Leninist theory. Many critics and political theorists have challenged the originality and/or orthodoxy of Mao Zedong's thought. But if Marxism is a theory of history, and communism that theory in political and social practice, then the one test of Mao's "authentic" Marxism is its success in practice, and few would deny that success. To transform in a lifetime the political system and social conditions of a quarter of mankind is arguably the greatest achievement in history. Mao did not bring it about single-handed, but his ideas and leadership were the major factor in the Chinese revolution. A biography of Mao Zedong is to a large extent a history of the Chinese Revolution.

P.R.

Youth

Mao Zedong was born in Shaoshan in Henan province, Central China, on 26 December 1893. He came from a peasant background but not, as is sometimes claimed, from a poor peasant family. His father, Mao Shunsheng, had begun life poor; however, after military service, by a combination of dealing in pigs and rice, money-lending and land-buying, he had become comparatively wealthy. The young Mao Zedong became leader of the greatest peasant-based revolution in history not so much through sympathies acquired with his mother's milk as in reaction against his acquisitive, self-made father.

Mao senior seems to have intended his eldest son to follow him in building the family fortunes through working their land, investing the profits, and, perhaps, acquiring status by contacts with the government. He sent his son to the local school in the hope that he would learn to read, write, and figure and when he was thirteen put him to work full time on the farm.

The young Mao had already displayed his rebelliousness at school. At one time, aged ten, he ran away after a beating. He himself admitted he was more interested in reading banned novels dealing with outlaws and rebellion than the classics, which were still the basic intellectual diet of Chinese schoolboys at the turn of the century. He used to read at night, hiding the lamp with a blanket, and sneak away from the fields during work hours. His father objected and accused him of laziness.

Matters came to a head in a clash from which, Mao much later told Edgar Snow, he learnt many lessons. In the presence of visitors, Mao's father cursed him and called him useless. Young Mao ran to the pond and threatened to commit suicide unless he got an apology. The dispute ended in a negotiated agreement: Mao Zedong agreed to *kotow* (bow) to his father — but on one knee only, not the normal full submission — in return for a promise that he would not be beaten. "I learned", he said, "that when I defended my rights by open rebellion my father relented, but when I remained meek and submissive he only cursed and beat me the more."

Other incidents from this period show Mao's awareness of the new ideas circulating in this last decade of the age-old empire. He read Zheng Guanying's *Words of Warning for an Affluent Age*, which had been published in the year of his birth. This was an eloquent and influential appeal for a reform programme of industrialization, military improvement, and political change. He also read pamphlets attacking the Japanese and other foreign intruders on China, which convinced him that China was in grave danger of destruction as an independent nation. Finally he absorbed some of the lessons of the social reformers of the time, whose ideas he read in the *New People's Journal*.

The foreigners were far away in the coastal ports, and a young peasant in an isolated village had little opportunity for rebellion against the Manchu government. But his father was near. When he was thirteen, Mao's parents arranged a marriage to a "suitable" nineteen-year-old girl, probably hoping to acquire some new unpaid labour. Mao absolutely refused to accept the bride he had no say in choosing. During the great Henan famines of 1906 and 1910, Mao sided with the poor tenants against his father. Finally, in 1910, against his father's wishes, he left home to return to primary school, a strapping young man of sixteen — an unusual decision reflecting an unusual youth.

We owe our knowledge of Mao as a child and youth mainly to his own reminiscences dictated to Edgar Snow in 1936 when Mao was already the leader of the Chinese Communist Party. Perhaps he exaggerated in retrospect the extent and cause of his struggles with his father. But he balanced that account with fond words for his mother. His mother seems to have been a kind, deeply religious woman, and although the mature Mao would not acknowledge it, he perhaps owed some of his later idealism and social activism to her Buddhist compassion and belief in an underlying purpose in the universe.

When Mao returned to school it was not to his own village's school but to the modern-style Dongshan Higher Primary School in the much larger town of Xiang-xiang, which his mother came from. This was to be the first step in an education pilgrimage that took him to the provincial capital, Changsha, and eventually the national capital, Beijing (Peking).

After a short time in this school, where he acquired a basic knowledge of history, geography, and science as well as developing his skills in writing Chinese, Mao successfully sat for the entrance examination of a high school in Changsha and arrived there in the autumn of 1911. He found himself introduced at one and the same time to city life and to politics, revolution, and war.

The 1911 school year had hardly begun when the Wuhan rising sparked off the nation-wide revolution that not only overthrew the Manchu dynasty but marked the end of the two-thousand-year-old Chinese monarchy. On 22 October the revolution spread to Henan. A new revolutionary provincial army was created. Mao Zedong, along with many other students, cut off his long queue, or pigtail, in defiance of the Beijing government and joined up.

By his own account, the political opinions of the eight-year-old Mao were republican and vaguely reformist. But the new government established in February 1912, with Yuan Shikai as president of the new republic, did not enlist his support. He left the army and began looking for a career.

The year 1912 was for Mao a period of drifting and uncertainty. In succession he was attracted to and abandoned the idea of training for the police, business, the law, even for soap-making. Finally, until his money ran out, he settled down to a solid course of self-education in the provincial library. He read Chinese translations of Darwin, Adam Smith, John Stuart Mill, Rousseau, and Spencer, as well as newspapers and history and geography. As he told Edgar Snow, it was in the Changsha library that for the first time he studied a map of the world.

Towards the end of his life, Mao said that he hoped to be known mainly as a teacher. The only career he ever pursued, besides that of politician, was teaching. But, like many people, he became a teacher by necessity. Just when his money ran out and his family was insisting that he settle down, he read an advertisement for the Henan First Normal School offering free tuition and cheap board to teacher trainees. His entrance essay was passed — as well as two others he wrote for friends — and in the spring of 1913 he began his course.

Mao continued his rebellion against authority at the school. He disliked having to study the physical sciences as well as the natural sciences and fought with his Chinese teacher, who disapproved of his modern writing style. Other more Westernized teachers saw promise in the difficult young man. One in particular, Yang Changji, who taught ethics, was to become a great influence on the life of his student. Mao was later to reject his philosophy but not his example of personal dedication, and he developed close personal ties, eventually marrying his daughter.

During the five years of his teacher-training course in Changsha, Mao Zedong began to show qualities of leadership. He led student expeditions into the mountains — "wind-bathing", as he called it. He advertised for like-minded male and female students to join him in working for their country, and the result was the formation of the New People's Study Society.

Many of the members of the new society were later to become leading members of the Chinese Communist party. In 1917, however, their programme was not one of political revolution but "to reform China and the world" by creating a nucleus of dedicated moral and social reformers among the youth. Their inspiration was the Shanghai-based periodical *New Youth* (subsequently based in Beijing), edited by Chen Duxiu, later to be the first Secretary-General of the Chinese Communist Party. They were opposed to Confucianism and the old ways; to foreign intrusion, especially Japanese; and to the warlords who seized power throughout China on the death of Yuan Shikai in the summer of 1916.

Some of the more perceptive leaders of the New Culture Movement — or New Thought Tide, as it later came to be called — recognized in the Bolshevik revolution in Russia in October 1917 a model that China might follow. But they were very ill-informed about Marxism until several years later. Mao was probably typical of the young Chinese of this period in his interests and activities. His first published work was "A Study of Physical Culture" in *New Youth* in April 1917, urging young Chinese to build strong bodies to place at the service of their country. "The principal aim of physical education is military heroism," he wrote. Later that year he put theory into practice when retreating troops attempted to commandeer the Normal School's dormitories. Using what was to become his typical tactics of planning, bluff, and surprise, Mao led his fellow students in an attack on the invaders and disarmed them.

Although he was not yet a Marxist socialist, during his last years in Changsha the young Mao seems to have seen the importance of contact with the workers. He persuaded the Student Society to develop a free night school for workers to teach reading, writing, and basic arithmetic, using the common vernacular rather than the difficult literary language as the medium. After several years in a student environment he was coming back to his roots.

When Mao graduated in May 1918 he was uncertain what to do. There was little point in returning home. Changsha under warlord rule was not attractive. Many of his fellow students were planning to go to France under a work-study programme and were going to Beijing to learn French. His beloved teacher Yang Changji was in Beijing, as were the leaders of the youth movement like Chen Duxiu, Hu Shi and Li Dazhao. So to Beijing he went. Less than a year later he returned to Changsha as a professional revolutionary.

The Young Revolutionary

It is significant that, despite his role as an organizer of the overseas study movement, Mao does not seem to have thought seriously of going abroad himself. The reason may have been partly his lack of facility in foreign languages; unlike, for example, Zhou Enlai, in later life he always used an interpreter. But much deeper was his fundamental "Chineseness". "I felt that I did not know enough about my own country," he said, "and that my time could be more profitably spent in China."

He began his search for the real China in Beijing, which was not only the political but the intellectual capital of China in 1918–19. He lived for a short time with Yang Changji, and it was probably at this time that he fell in love with Yang's daughter, Yang Kaihui. He soon moved into a squalid single room in old Beijing which he shared with seven others. Yang, who was now a professor at the Peita (Beijing University), introduced him to Li Dazhao, Professor of History and the university librarian, who found him a job as assistant librarian. This job not only gained him contacts in the university but introduced him to the study groups led by Li which were seriously studying socialist and anarchist ideas.

Mao seemed to have been more attracted at first to anarchism and romantic revolutionary ideas than to Marxist economic and social theory. Perhaps we can see the personal roots of his new-found vocation as a radical revolutionary in some bitter remarks to Edgar Snow about the attitude of Beijing intellectuals to a young, half-educated provincial speaking Henanese dialect. "To most of them," he said, "I didn't exist as a human being. . . . I tried to begin conversations with them on political and cultural subjects, but they were very busy men. They had no time to listen to an assistant librarian speaking southern dialect." Much of his later distaste for intellectuals and theorists, for experts and bureaucrats, appear in these words.

Mao's unofficial education course in "The Green Forest

University, the school of hard knocks" continued in early 1919 with a long, roundabout journey from Beijing to Shanghai and eventually back to Henan. He visited the gave and birthplace of Confucius and climbed Taishan, the sacred mountain; he saw for the first time the battlefields that had inspired him as a boy when he read the *Romance of the Three Kingdoms*; and he toured the southern capital, Nanjing. These are the highlights of his trip as he later recalled them, suggesting again the youthful romantic rather than the professional revolutionary.

Nevertheless his return to Changsha marks the real beginning of his political career. His job as a primary school teacher seems to have had little interest for him. He resumed leadership of the New People's Study Society and plunged into new activities aimed against the military governor of Henan, Zhang Jingyao.

In May 1919 there began an outburst of patriotic indignation against the decisions of the Versailles Peace Conference to grant former German concessions in China to the Japanese. Known as the May Fourth Movement, after the Beijing student demonstrations on that day, it quickly spread through the major cities of China. Numerous new periodicals sprang up, among them the Changsha *Hsiang River Review*, which was founded, edited, and mostly written by Mao Zedong. Mao's solution to the problems of the world was a "union of communist republics" achieved through organization of the peasants and workers. However, the weakness of his own organizational base was soon shown when the Governor suppressed his paper.

As part of the campaign against Zhang Jingyao, Mao was sent to Beijing in January 1920 to secure support of the student groups there. This brief visit was of crucial importance in his conversion to Marxism. He read the *Communist Manifesto*, which had just been translated into Chinese, as well as Kautsky's *Class Struggle* and a history of socialism. His return journey by way of Shanghai enabled him again to meet Chen Duxiu, who was himself in the process of abandoning Western liberalism for Marxism-Leninism. Mao was deeply depressed.

In July 1920 Mao was able to return to Changsha in triumph. Zhang Jingyao had been driven out by rival warlords. In the turn of the political dice a friend had become director of the First Normal School and had asked Mao Zedong to be the principal of the primary school attached to it. He now had political influence and a steady income and could marry Yang Kaihui, whose father had recently died.

Mao was by now a Marxist but not strictly a communist, since there was no communist party in China as yet. Groups of students and intellectuals had begun the process of forming a Chinese Communist Party (CCP), and Mao played a leading role in Henan. He set up a left-wing bookshop, organized a Russian affairs study group, and sometime later in 1920 organized a "communist group" which was the nucleus of the Henan branch of the CCP. Other groups in Shanghai, Beijing, and Paris (where Zhou Enlai and Li Lisan were students) were similarly forming, and formal contact had been made by Chen Duxiu with the Third International.

By mid-1921 there were six communist groups in China and the time had come to formally create the Chinese Communist Party. A congress was called for Shanghai to meet on 1 July. Two delegates came from each group, and Mao Zedong was one of the Henan delegates. The meeting was held in a girls' school, closed for the summer holidays, in the French Concession, which was thought to be safer than the Chinese city. Even there they were disturbed by a suspected spy and had to hold their last session on a boat on a lake in a nearby resort.

The policies of the infant CCP adopted at the First Congress were the orthodox Marxist policies of worker-led urban-based revolution. It is sometimes claimed that even then, in 1921, Mao Zedong disapproved of this emphasis on the proletariat, but there is no evidence for this view. It is much more likely that he went along with the Russian-inspired line proposed by the Comintern representatives, Voitinsky and Maring. Furthermore, Mao was one of the most junior members of the congress and, despite his appointment as secretary of the Henan branch of the new party, was not taken very seriously by the big-city intellectuals who led the party. Chen Duxiu became the Secretary-General, and party headquarters were established in Shanghai, China's largest and most industrialized city. The first task of the Henan and other branches was to organize trade unions among the workers.

The year 1922 saw a series of strikes and labour unrest in which the CCP played a part. The most important of them, the Anyuan miners' strike, has often been presented as inspired and led by Mao Zedong, but it seems likely that his fellow Henanese Liu Shaoqi and Li Lisan were more directly involved. This is a good example of the problems involved in determining Mao's precise role in events. Both Liu and Li later fell foul of Mao and became "non persons" and so had to be expunged from the record. Actually the CCP was so small at the time that it is only in hindsight that its influence can be seen as significant.

A much more important development for the future of the Chinese Revolution was the reorganization of the Guomindang (Kuomintang, or KMT), the Nationalist Party, by Sun Yatsen. The Russians and the Comintern saw this as the best hope for China and urged the CCP to join them in a united front. This became official policy at the Second Congress of the CCP in July 1922. Mao did not attend this meeting. His own account is the highly improbable one that he forgot the address and could not find the meeting place. More likely he was out of sympathy with the party's leadership, or they with him.

By the Third Congress of the CCP held in Canton in June 1923, Mao had healed whatever breach may have existed between him and the Central Committee of the party. He enthusiastically supported the policy of co-operation with the KMT, including handing over control of his precious labour organizations. Mao was elected to the Central Committee and made head of the important Organization Bureau, replacing Zang Guotao, who was to become perhaps his most bitter enemy within the party. Shortly after, he became a member of the Central Executive Committee of the reorganized KMT and hence one of the key links between the two parties. For the next few years Mao was to be far more prominent in Nationalist than Communist circles, using KMT organizations as his field of action.

The KMT/CCP United Front of 1923–27 was to prove in the end a disaster for the Communists, but it brought many immediate benefits. Apart from Russian experience in party-building, it gave the revolutionaries an army well trained and dedicated to the overthrow of the warlords and expulsion of the imperialists. Sun Yatsen was an acceptable leader to both sides, his early death could not have been predicted. Jiang Jie-shi (Chiang Kai-shek) who was to succeed him as KMT leader, was commonly labelled in this period the "Red General"; he had spent some time in Moscow, and his political commissar at the Whampoa Military Academy was Zhou Enlai, who could be relied upon to turn the minds of the officer corps towards revolutionary goals. The success of the policy can be seen in the fact that membership of the party grew in a few years to some fifty thousand.

Mao spent most of 1924 in Shanghai in the dual role of CCP organizer and member of the Shanghai bureau of the KMT. It is clear that he was still deeply committed to a revolution based in the cities, and it was chance that led him to reassess the revolutionary possibilities of the countryside. It would appear that his leading role in the United Front had caused some bitter attacks on Mao by hard-line Communists like Li Lisan. Mao, whether diplomatically or actually ill from the strain, returned to his native Shaoshan to recuperate late in 1924 and found there a great change in the attitudes of the peasants. His new-found interest in the peasants was to alienate him further from CCP leadership; he was, for example, dropped from the Central Committee. But his experiences with the Henan peasantry were to shape the successful revolutionary strategy that led him and the party to victory a generation later.

Mao and Revolution in the Countryside

It may seem strange that a peasant boy like Mao Zedong should have come so late to appreciate the potential of the peasantry in achieving his double aim of driving out the foreign imperialists and building a new society in China. However, he had been away from the farm for many years; he had absorbed many of the educated Chinese prejudices against the man who dirties his hands; and these prejudices had been reinforced by the Marxist view that peasants were too unorganized and too attached to their land to readily become communists.

Nor was Mao Zedong the first Communist to organize among the peasants. Peng Pai, as early as 1922, had created peasants' unions in Hailufeng in coastal Guangdong and had created a peasant training institute in Canton under KMT auspices. The Comintern, too, was beginning to urge greater use of peasant agitation in the underdeveloped countries of Asia.

Perhaps Mao's most marked characteristic was his ability to learn from personal experience. Theory was to be used to organize and formulate that experience, but practice came first. In late 1924 and 1925 Mao discovered that peasant revolution could work. Although he later claimed to have "organized the nucleus of the great peasant movement" of Henan, even by his own account the peasants led the way and he followed. Soon, however, the governor of Henan heard of his activities and ordered his arrest. Mao fled to Canton, where the KMT was poised to begin its Northern Expedition to conquer the warlords of central and northern China.

In Canton Mao Zedong was once more mainly associated with the left wing of the Guomindang. He worked as director of the Political Department under Wang Jingwei and edited its *Political Weekly*. Now, however, he took a new and special interest in the Peasant Movement Training Institute, which was training organizers to work in the countryside. He encouraged Henanese Communists, including his own younger brother,

Mao Zemin, to join the institute, and personally conducted its sixth session beginning in May 1926.

We can get an insight into Mao's thinking at this time by reading his "Analysis of the Classes in Chinese Society", published in March 1926, and his February 1927 "Report of an Investigation into the Peasant Movement in Henan", his first important theoretical essays. Their full significance was not appreciated at the time, and their originality (or unorthodoxy, to take the viewpoint of his party opponents) has been masked by later amendments to the official versions. Mao did not, in 1926-27, assign the leading role in the Chinese Revolution to the urban workers. He thought of the peasants as rising spontaneously and irresistibly:

> In a very short time, several hundred million peasants in China's central, southern, and northern provinces will rise like a tornado or tempest — a force so extraordinarily swift and violent that no power, however great, will be able to suppress it. . . . all revolutionary parties and all revolutionary comrades will stand before them to be tested, to be accepted or rejected by them. To march at their head and lead them? To follow in the rear, gesticulating at them, and criticizing them? [From "Report of an Investigation"]

Chen Duxiu and his colleagues did not fail to see the barbed reference to their concentration on the cities in the last comment. Mao was now even further out of favour with the Central Committee of the CCP. But meanwhile their own policies were being tested. Sun Yatsen had died unexpectedly on a trip to Beijing in March 1925. Jiang Jie-shi (Chiang Kai-shek) had emerged as the strongman of the KMT and was showing signs of repudiating the United Front. In April 1927, as the KMT armies occupied Shanghai, Jiang massacred the Communists and left-wing unionists who have paved the way for his success.

It was, then, in a crisis atmosphere that the Fifth Congress of the CCP met in the industrial city of Wuhan in central China in May 1927. Mao and his supporters from the peasant movement urged full support for the rural revolution and an acceleration of the confiscation of the land held by landlords and rich peasants. It is interesting to note that he drew the line at thirty *mou* (about 1.8 hectares), a little more than his father had owned. But Mao's measures were in the end not adopted, mainly, it seems, out of fear that sympathetic officers in the revolutionary army, many of whom came from landlord families, would be alienated.

Why were the CCP leaders still so concerned about offending KMT members and supporters after the events of April in Shanghai? The reason lies partly in the policies of Stalin. He had advocated the United Front strategy in China against the opposition of Trotsky. To change it now would be to admit he had been wrong, and his representative, Borodin, strongly opposed any change. On the other hand the "Left" KMT leaders in Wuhan, such as Wang Jingwei, still adhered to the KMT/CCP alliance. Jiang Jie-shi might have the army, but Wang and his colleagues were still the official leaders of the revolutionary government.

By the end of May, Stalin seems to have realized that the situation was desperate. He sent a telegram urging in effect a Communist takeover of the KMT Central Committee and the creation of a new Communist Party army. For reasons never adequately explained, the Indian Comintern representative, M.N. Roy, showed the telegram to Wang Jingwei, who took fright and by July 1927 had re-established the ties between the Wuhan government and Jiang Jie-shi.

The Communists now had no choice but open rebellion. In late 1927 they staged a series of risings in the cities where they had influence, all of which were utter failures. Mao himself organized one in Henan, timed for the autumn harvest period, and aimed at capturing Changsha using an army composed partly of former KMT troops and partly of peasant and worker militiamen. Zhou Enlai, Zhu De, and others engineered the Nanchang rising in August; it ended in a retreat to Guangdong in which all discipline in the army broke down. Finally Stalin personally ordered the most disastrous of them all, the Canton rising of December.

During the autumn harvest rising, Mao came closer to death than perhaps at any time in his career. He was captured by the enemy, fortunately militia rather than regular troops. He managed to bribe the soldiers to let him go, but their sergeant refused to release him. Then, just two hundred metres from their headquarters, which he was unlikely to leave alive in those days of the "white terror", he broke loose. He hid in the reeds by a pond and slipped off to the hills at nightfall. This sort of experience was common at the time. Few of the Communist leaders avoided close shaves. Most lost family and friends, as Mao was to lose his wife, Yang Kaihui, and sister a few years later. This debt of blood goes far to explaining the ferocity of the Communists in later days. "Revolution", said Mao, "is not a dinner party."

Although (or perhaps because) it was clear that the 1927 risings had been hopeless from the beginning, the Central Committee of the CCP sought scapegoats. In November Mao was removed from all his party posts, accused of disobeying orders in calling off the attack on Changsha, and "military opportunism". Once more, Mao learned from experience. He had found the professional soldiers politically unreliable and the dedicated militia untrained. Those still loyal he withdrew to the Jinggangshan mountains on the border between Henan and Jiangxi, a traditional bandit stronghold, and devoted himself to the creation of a Red Army that would be both committed and efficient.

The period that Mao Zedong spent in the Janggangshan base area laid the foundations of his political ascendancy in the CCP. He was remote from the Central Committee and could claim, often truthfully, that their instructions had not reached him. He was outside direct control from Moscow and hence not involved in the ideological disputes and recriminations that inevitably erupted in the following years. And he had an opportunity to test his military and economic theories in an isolated and relatively safe rural area. A debacle for the CCP turned into a personal triump for Mao Zedong.

Once enough territory had been brought under control, Mao established a soviet self-governing area controlled by an elected People's Council with its capital at Zhalin. As further remnants of the defeated revolutionary armies struggled in, including the best troops commanded by Zhu De, Chen Yi, and Lin Biao, they were consolidated into a new Fourth Army under Zhu De, with Mao as political commissar. Later a Fifth Army was added, led by Peng Dehuai. A radical land-confiscation policy was adopted, although as further soviets were established a more moderate policy was adopted towards the smaller landowners who co-operated with the Communists. One of the most effective tactics adopted by the soviet governments was to insist on the observance of the Nationalist law restricting rent to 37½ per cent of the produce, which had not been seriously applied in the KMT-controlled areas.

Nevertheless, the position of the Communists was precarious. As their forces grew, the bare mountain fields could not produce enough to feed them, even with the labour of all hands. They were short of essentials like salt, ill armed, and constantly harassed by KMT armies. Their only safety lay in breaking through the encirclement and extending their territory. Given their lesser numbers, fixed battles were to be avoided. Mao's troops became adept at guerrilla tactics — sudden attacks in strength, retreat before advancing armies, mobility and flexibility. They relied on the support of the peasants — like fish in the sea, as Mao put it.

In early 1929 Mao and Zhu De struck south-east into southern Jiangxi province and, after losing nearly half their army, found a safer home in Ruijin, which became the capital of the Chinese Soviet Republic. They were still far from secure — one of their centres, Jian, was lost and recaptured nine times in 1930 — but they were able to concentrate on the political education and reorganization of their men. During the previous three years the Central Committee, now led by Li Lisan, had sniped at Mao's policies and even removed him from formal control of the soviet at least once, but they could not deny that his line was working and theirs of urban revolution failing. Now an uneasy peace was made. Mao was acknowledged as head of the Jiangxi soviet, while he in return paid lip service to the proletarian revolution, although it is hard to see where the proletarians were to be found in his motley crew of professional soldiers, ex-bandits, and peasants.

Mao's growing confidence in the correctness of his ideas is seen in his report "On the Rectification of Incorrect Ideas in the Party" (December 1929), in which he attacked "adventurism" in the party — that is, blind and irresolute support of urban risings. Li Lisan's adventurism was not yet over. He rejected Mao's "boxing tactics" and urged one last blow at the brains and hearts of the government, the cities. The Red Army, some seventy thousand strong now, was to be regrouped into three army corps to attack the large cities of south and central China. Mao and Zhu De's first Army Corps were to attack Nanchang; the Second were to move against Wuhan, while Peng Dehuai's Third attacked Changsha. When the attacks were launched in June 1930, only Changsha fell to the Communists, and it was held for ten days only.

The failure of the 1930 summer campaign inevitably led to Li Lisan's disgrace. The Comintern sent a group of young Moscow-trained leaders, usually referred to as the "Twenty-eight Bolsheviks", to take control of the CCP. But directions from

Shanghai, and (even more) Moscow, were now even less likely to be heeded. Mao Zedong and Zhu De retreated to their base area thoroughly convinced that the future of the party lay in the countryside. However it was not to be in south-east China.

Jiang Jie-shi appears to have been shocked by the near success of the Communists in taking Changsha. Despite a growing problem with the Japanese in Manchuria, he determined to throw all his military resources into blockading and crushing the Communists. They were a disease of the heart, he declared, while the Japanese were merely a skin disease. So began the first of five encirclement campaigns that were to end in the Red Army being forced out of Jiangxi.

In late 1930 occurred one of the most crucial but still mysterious events in Mao's rise to power. In a complex series of manoeuvres against his remaining opponents within the Jiangxi soviet, Mao had several thousand men arrested as suspected KMT agents at Fudien, and provoked a mutiny which brought to light his enemies. There is strong suspicion that Mao used *agents provocateurs* to brand some of his intra-party opponents as secret members of the KMT or the Anti-Bolshevik Corps. It is alleged that several thousand soldiers and party members were killed in Mao's counter coup. Certainly the CCP central committee was far from satisfied with Mao's explanation, while Zhu De, who objected to thus losing so many key military personnel, was estranged from Mao for a time. But Mao had achieved his ends. He and his followers now had control of both the soviet government and the party apparatus in Jiangxi.

As the KMT encirclement campaigns proceeded, however, Mao once again came under attack, this time for his guerrilla military tactics. Zhou Enlai, backed by Wang Ming, now in control of the Central Committee, which had moved to Jiangxi, successfully halted the advancing KMT army in February 1933 by a concentrated attack rather than retreating as Mao advocated. Mao claimed he was ill and retired to convalesce, as he had done in the past and would do again in the future. Mao's mysterious illnesses are a subject more for the psychiatrist than the historian, but they suggest at least a curiously sensitive nature for a revolutionary leader capable, as we have seen, of decisive and ruthless action.

The fifth encirclement campaign, beginning in late 1933, was to prove the crucial one. Jiang Jie-shi had reorganized his forces with the aid of a German military adviser, General Hans von

Seeckt. This time they proceeded much more cautiously, clearing suspect villages on the fringes of the Red area and building a ring of blockhouses and new roads for troop transport. Smuggling into the soviet area almost ceased, and vital supplies were cut off. Once again Mao was overruled on strategy, and a series of fierce battles followed in which the Red Army was little by little worn down. By October 1934 the Communists decided that had no choice but to break down and abandon the base area. On 16 October about a hundred thousand men and women (including Mao's second wife), He Zizhen began the retreat from Jiangxi.

The Long March

The Long March which thus began is justly famous as the great epic event in CCP history. In just over a year Mao's main force, the First Front Army, covered on foot about 9,600 kilometres, a journey longer than that from Sydney to Perth and return. They went through almost every conceivable terrain from tropical south to icy northern steppes, crossed several great rivers and numerous mountain ranges, perished from cold in high passes, and were sucked into the swamp of the grasslands. Only a fraction — some estimates say five thousand — endured to the end, although not all died or were killed on the way. Many simply merged into the peasant population to continue the fight underground.

In retrospect, the move to the north-west of China is seen to be the key to the Communist victory fifteen years later. There they could mount a "national" defence against the Japanese without directly facing the main Japanese armies in the coastal areas. The landowners of the north, where absentee landlordism was less rife, felt less threatened by the CCP's land policies, and they were able to build up their strength under less threat from the KMT armies, which were concentrated in the eastern cities. But although Mao claimed that this had been his intention from the beginning, it would seem that the destination, Shaanxi, was more or less accident. The course of the march was dictated by the strength and location of their enemies. Jiang Jie-shi's description of the march in his memoirs as "Communist Bandits' Flight Westwards" is not far from the truth.

The argument over Mao's plans in October 1934 is in any case largely irrelevant. During the fifth encirclement and the conference that decided on the march, Mao Zedong was not in control of CCP policy-making. When the army set out, Zhu De was in command (advised by the German Comintern military expert Otto Braun) and Zhou Enlai was the political commissar. Mao had been seriously ill with malaria in August and

September, and some of his opponents claim that he was virtually under arrest. It was only during and partly as a result of the Long March that Mao Zedong finally achieved supreme power in the Chinese Communist Party.

The Communist forces set out initially in a north-westerly direction, apparently hoping to join another army group under Ho Lung in north-west Henan. But this direct route led to a disaster in crossing the Xiang River, when about half the Red Army was lost during a week's bitter fighting. Otto Braun, whose strategy was responsible, was discredited; Mao began to take charge, changing the direction of the march westward. In mountainous Guizhou they halted, and at a conference in Zunyi the Politburo of the CCP appointed Mao Zedong chairman of the Military Council. Luo Fu was elected as party secretary, but the party was now in effect an army on the march and "Chairman Mao" was in charge. From this decision on 8 January 1935 until his death, Mao Zedong was the clear, although not unchallenged, leader of the party.

The difficulties of the march, as well as something of the exhilaration, is forcefully expressed in poems written at the time by Mao:

> They tell us that the pass is strong as iron.
> Yet today in one giant step we will cross it.
> We will get through these hills, blue as the
> sea, while the sun sets blood-red.
>   ["On Crossing the Loushan Pass", January 1935]

And a little later, in the mountains of the far West:

> Mountains!
> I spur my horse on, unable to dismount,
> While if I look up the sky is only a few feet
> above me.
> Mountains!
> Rolling like the waves of some stormy sea,
> Like a thousand war-horses rearing and plunging in battle.

These and other poems of Mao's give us tantalizing glimpses of the inner self concealed beneath the public man. They have sometimes been disparaged as traditional in form and conventional in sentiment, but it is hard to read some of them at least without being moved.

Mao's study of traditional Chinese military tactics, began to pay off. When Jiang Jie-shi's troops blocked the way to Yunnan he doubled back towards Guiyang, the capital of Guizhou, forcing Jiang, who was personally in command there, to call up the Yunnan garrisons in reinforcement. Mao's men then seized the ferry point at the provincial border crossing on the Jinsha River and advanced northwards through Yunnan.

Jiang Jie-shi, who had been thus foiled of his prey, flew northwards to Chongqing, capital of Sichuan, to deliver what he thought would be the final blow. The Dadu (or Tatu) River to the west of Sichuan, with its deep gorges and rapids, formed a perfect natural barrier. Jiang expected to confine the Red Army to the mountains of Xikang, bordering on Tibet, where his air force, combined with the terrain and lack of supplies, would finally defeat his old enemy.

Once again Mao's military genius appeared. At Luding, on the Dadu, a suspension bridge made of iron chains with wooden flooring spanned the gorge. It was heavily guarded at the eastern (Sichuan) end. If the Red Army could capture the bridge they could cross in safety. Small parties could cross by boat lower down, but the whole army would take too long to cross and be exposed to air attack.

Mao ordered the First Division to cross by ferry while the main force drove up the left bank. The advance group was given just two days to cover 170 kilometres along the cliffs above the Dadu gorge. This ploy caught the garrison defending the bridge unprepared. On the afternoon of 25 May, a commando group crossed hand over hand along the iron chains — the planks had been removed on their side — and, with heavy losses, secured the bridge approaches. The First Division joined them and the entire army crossed into Sichuan.

Once in Sichuan Mao faced political as well as military difficulties. Here was the stronghold of Zhang Guotao, another party veteran and longtime rival of Mao. After Mao's First Front Army had joined up with Zhang's Fourth Front Army, there was a serious disagreement over their ultimate destination. Zhang wanted to go westwards towards the Tibetan border and safety; Mao proposed the Shaanxi-Kansu border area to the north, arguing that the time was ripe to exploit the nationalism aroused by the Japanese invasion of China's northern provinces. They could not agree, and each set out in his favoured direction. Even Zhu De went with Zhang Guotao, although he afterwards claimed to have been forced to do so.

The last and shortest stage of the Long March for Mao's First Army into Kansu and Shaanxi proved to be perhaps the most difficult of all, even though Jiang Jie-shi left them alone at last. Their course now lay through the grasslands, a vast area of swamps inhabited by hostile tribesmen who deprived the Red Army of food supplies, harassed them at every opportunity, and led them astray. Starving, ill from the diet, mud, and chilling rain, they struggled out into the loess plains of north China. In October 1935, Mao's forces arrived in the base area on the Kansu-Shaanxi border to join the seven-thousand-strong Fifteenth Army Corps which held it. Next year Ho Lung's Henan army, and finally Zhang Guotao and Zhu De, reinforced them; Yan'an (Yenan) in north-west Shaanxi became their capital, and the Yan'an era began.

The Yan'an Years

At the end of the Long March, in December 1935, Chairman Mao called a meeting of the Politburo (the Political Bureau of the Central Committee of the CCP) to discuss future policies. In his report, later published as "On Tactics against Japanese Imperialism", he commented on the success of the march.

> Has history ever witnessed a long march such as ours? For twelve months we were under daily reconnaissance and bombing from the skies by scores of planes, while on land we were encircled and pursued, obstructed and intercepted by a huge force of several hundred thousand men, and we encountered untold difficulties and dangers on the way; yet by using our two legs we swept across a distance of more than twenty thousand li through the length and breadth of eleven provinces.

The march, he said, had been a triumph for the Red Army, had brought the Communists to the attention of eleven provinces of China, and had sown the seeds of a future victory. Now, said Mao, is the time for patience and new tactics. We must form a broad revolutionary national united front with all those who share our aims of driving out the Japanese imperialists, including even those who are not interested in social revolution or are friendly to the European and American imperialists. Eventually conditions will be ripe for the transition to a socialist revolution; for the moment democratic national revolution must be our aim.

The general political line, then, was to be one of a renewed united front with the KMT against the Japanese. The snag was, of course, that Jiang Jie-shi would have none of it. It was a further year before the Xi'an Incident occurred, in which Jiang's own army placed him under arrest until he agreed to fight the Japanese rather than the Communists.

Meanwhile, Mao Zedong concentrated on rebuilding the Red Army, reorganizing and purifying the party, and carrying out social and economic reform in the Red areas. This was the first real experience of government of an extended and various area that the CCP had had. We can discern in the experiments of the Yan'an period — the "Yenan Way", as Mark Selden calls it — the outline of the later People's Republic of China. The CCP did not have to come to power, as many revolutionary regimes have had to, untried and untrained in government. By 1949 they had a large corps of experienced administrators as well as an army and a disciplined party organization.

Since the army was the basis of CCP power, it is the Red Army (later to be called the PLA — People's Liberation Army) that we should study first. In many respects it is an error to distinguish the army strongly from the party. It was in the fullest sense a party army. Its tasks were political and civil as much as military. Its leaders and many of its ordinary soldiers were party members.

The Red Army was seen as a people's army. Like all Chinese armies, its recruits were mainly peasants. But they sought, unlike most other Chinese armies, to be with and of the people. The eight rules for the army, formulated in 1928, summed up their differences from KMT and warlord armies. The Red Army was ordered to be courteous and helpful to the civilian population, not to take what they needed but to pay for it. Of necessity, given the shortage of armaments and their inferior strength, they had to rely on morale and tactics for success. The morale and discipline came from constant political indoctrination. The tactics were those of small mobile groups, uniting for sudden attacks and slipping away to avoid destruction by conventional forces.

> When the enemy advances, we retreat!
> When the enemy halts, we harass them!
> When the enemy avoids battle, we attack!
> When the enemy retreats, we pursue!

After the establishment of the capital in Yan'an, and especially after the Japanese attack on Beijing in July 1937, which quickly spread to the whole of east China, the Communist border region became a Mecca for young Chinese. The North-West Anti-Japanese Red Army University, set up in April 1936, and the Lu Xun Academy for Literature and the Arts, named after the Leftist (but non-Communist) writer Lu Xun, attracted intellectuals and artists from the great coastal cities like Shanghai, Beijing, and Canton. Among them was a pretty young Shanghai actress, Lan Ping, better known as Jiang Qing, who became Mao's third wife. (He Zizhen, who had been injured in an air raid during the Long March, was sent to Moscow for medical treatment.)

This influx of enthusiastic youngsters, as well as the extension of the party through the villages and towns under Communist control, brought a huge influx of new members into the CCP. From forty thousand in 1937, its numbers grew to eight hundred thousand by 1940. There were tensions between the Long March veterans and the newcomers, who were often much better educated. What came to be known as the "Red or Expert" debate arose for the first time. Should redness or expertise be heeded in decision-making?

Mao Zedong relished the resumption of his old role of teacher towards these newcomers. Edgar Snow described Mao in 1936, after years of ceaseless activity, happily settling down to philosophical studies, reading new books on Marxism, including the theoretical writings of Stalin, and working often through the night on his own writings. There appeared during the year 1937 to 1945 a series of important theoretical statements from his pen: "On Practice" and "On Contradiction" (1937), "On New Democracy" (1940), "Talks at the Yan'an Forum on Literature and Art" (1942), "On Coalition Government", and "The Foolish Old Man who Removed the Mountains" (1945).

It is to these and other works of the period that the experts who debate the nature and originality of Maoism as a political doctrine mainly appeal. This emphasis may, as we have earlier seen, be wrong. Mao's originality lies much more in practice than in the extension and elaboration of Marxist theory. But in these works he did develop a consistent theoretical basis for his innovations in and applications of Marxism to Chinese conditions. In October 1938 he wrote of Marxism being given "a national form" which he called "concrete Marxism" or "the sinification of Marxism". He himself never claimed for his ideas the status of an "ism", as in Marxism, Leninism, and Stalinism. Rather his ideas were *Mao Zedong Sixiang*, the thought — or better, the thinking — of Mao Zedong. This thinking, this constant weighing of political and social conditions, was a never-ending process leading to changes in emphasis, new campaigns, and so forth.

We can, however, detect certain characteristic themes in Mao's thinking that recur in his writings and in the intra-party and national campaigns under his leadership. First there is an emphasis on conflict, struggle, strife. The theoretical basis of this is his theory of contradiction, as expressed in 1937 and in developed form in 1957 and during the Cultural Revolution of the late 1960s. "If there were no contradictions and no struggle, there would be no world, no progress, no life, there would be nothing at all", was how the mature Mao put it in 1958 at the Chengtu Conference. The language is that of Marxism-Leninism, but, as many observers have noted, it also owes much to the traditional Chinese ideas of *yin* and *yang*, the constant flux of the balance of forces in the universe. Others have detected not a little sheer love of mischief-making in Mao.

Closely connected wtih this and arising out of it is a second theme, that of continuous revolution. The struggle must never cease. There is no final victory. Even in a socialist society from which the counter-revolutionaries have been eliminated there are still "non-antagonistic contradictions" to be struggled against; hence the recurrent political campaigns since 1950, the build-up of tension and then its release, that have kept China watchers fascinated. "To rebel is justified," Mao told the Red Guards. Revolution for Mao was almost an end in itself, morally and spiritually purifying. Those who had not gone through the Long March or experienced the Civil War must make revolution against their elders.

Yet a third connected theme was Mao's suspicion of bureaucrats, of intellectuals, of élites. When hard pressed by party officials who told him his policies were unpractical, theoretically incorrect, or dangerous, Mao several times appealed directly to the ordinary people, the peasants and workers, the young. His language could be earthy, even coarse, as some of the remarks collected by Stuart Schram in *Mao Tse-tung Unrehearsed* reveal. They were certainly offensive to the party intellectuals. But Mao never forgot, as they often did, that China was a nation of peasants. He insisted that all must get their hands dirty, must "learn from the workers". In Yan'an all were expected to do some manual work. Mao himself grew tobacco, perhaps in consciously ironic reference to his chain-smoking habit. The May 7 Cadre Schools of the Cultural Revolution, where bureaucrats went back to the land, were not really an innovation but a return to one of Mao Zedong's most deeply held convictions.

The first of the great intra-party campaigns inspired by Mao to implement his ideas was the Rectification Campaign of 1941-43 in Yan'an. Party members had to correct their work style by study, self-criticism, and inner struggle. They had to expose themselves to the criticism of others in special small-group meetings. The aim was to change one's ideas and way of acting. Those who resisted change were purged from the party.

During the Yan'an years, Mao consolidated his personal control of the party apparatus. Zhang Guotao, whose influence had waned after his divergences during the Long March, was brought back into the government in 1937, but he took advantage of a KMT mission to Yan'an in April 1938 to escape to the Nationalist zone and eventually to Hong Kong. He spent much of the rest of his life writing his memoirs and taking every opportunity to smear the reputation of his old and successful rival. Wang Ming was sent back from Moscow in early 1938 in an attempt to assert Comintern control over Mao, but he too failed to wrest power from the chairman. At the Seventh Party Congress in 1945 the party constitution was rewritten and Mao was elected unopposed to the new position of chairman of the Central Committee of the CCP. Wang Ming was another who ended his life in exile — as Moscow's chief spokesman against Mao Zedong's "revisionism".

Reform of the army and of the party were two major achievements of the Yan'an years. But the main task remained — to win the nation. We will look shortly at the military victories against the Japanese and the Nationalists. These would, however, have been impossible without the CCP's success in winning the minds and hearts of the people. During the anti-Japanese war, from 1937 to 1945, the Communists succeeded in extending their territory at the expense of both the Japanese and the Nationalists. In these new areas, as in the old, they set up governments that for the duration of the war pursued moderate national-unity policies and convinced many Chinese and foreign observers that they offered an attractive alternative to the KMT. The governments were not exclusively Communist, although certainly dominated by the Communists; they were formally tripartite — composed of one-third CCP members, one-third left-wing non-Communists, and one-third independent. They proclaimed democracy and, in the sense of representation and participation in decision-making, practised it. Their long-term aim of "dictatorship of the proletariat" was not disavowed but put off into the future.

Land policy, too, was moderate. Some large landowners, especially those who could be accused of collaboration with the Japanese, were dispossessed. But in place of large-scale land redistribution, the Communists insisted on strict limitation of land rent to around a third of the crop. Landowners, especially if they worked their own land, were guaranteed their rent. Once again, the eventual distribution of land to the landless was promised to attract the poor, while the rich were appeased by a go-slow policy.

Production drives were inaugurated with rewards for the model workers and units. Rations, which were severely limited both for officials and soldiers because of Japanese and KMT pressure, were eventually increased to above pre-war levels. New small industries were set up using locally made, improvised machinery to provide goods previously imported from the coastal cities or abroad. Self-sufficiency was the aim, and it was often achieved.

At the same time the party and government organs were, after July 1941, linked more closely to the people through the "to-the-villages" movement. Students and cadres were sent to the countryside to help in the harvest and, later, assigned temporarily to lend their technical and cultural skills to the villagers. The great gap between city and country was lessened; the peasants lost some of their suspicion of government officials; and communist planners gained first-hand experience of rural conditions and attitudes.

Their successes in government were modest enough, but in wartime conditions, and in contrast to what was happening in the KMT-controlled areas, they were convincing. Inflation was a problem, but by 1944 it was under control in the Red areas. In the Nationalist areas it was a hefty 300 per cent per annum in the last years of the war, with the usual consequences of loss of morale and alienation of the group most essential to the government — the public servants, teachers, army officers, and businessmen.

Nevertheless, it was essentially the success of the CCP in building its image as the true nationalists, the true defenders of Chinese territory and people against the Japanese, that enabled them to grow as a deadly rival and challenge the KMT for government in 1945.

The Anti-Japanese War

Japan had invaded Manchuria in 1931 and established a puppet Manchukuo state. This was, of course, bitterly resisted by the inhabitants of Manchuria; but for a while it seemed as if the Japanese had no ambitions beyond securing Manchurian mineral resources, and the Chinese government tried to avoid provoking further trouble. So too the League of Nations and the outside world.

Jiang Jie-shi resisted attempts to embroil him with the Japanese until December 1936. He had flown to Xi'an, capital of Shaanxi, to meet Zhang Xueliang, leader of the Manchurian exile forces, but instead of agreeing to help free their homeland, he announced yet another drive against the nearby Communists. Marshall Zhang and the local commander, Yang Hucheng, rebelled and placed Jiang Jie-shi under arrest in an attempt to force him to move against the Japanese.

While the CCP did not initiate the Xi'an incident, they were quick to take advantage of it. It must have been very tempting to get rid of their old enemy, whom they regarded as personally responsible for the murders of so many of their family and friends. Both Mao and Zhou Enlai told Westerners that this was one of the hardest decisions they ever had to make. As disciplined Communists, however, they had no choice. Jiang was the only possible leader of a general war of resistance. After negotiations, and Zhang Xueliang's arrest to save face, Jiang tacitly agreed to the demands of his soldiers. And so the Second United Front was launched.

During early 1937 the terms of an agreement were worked out. The main points were that the CCP should abandon all attempts to oust the Nationalist government; that in return the KMT would recognize the Shaanxi border area as a "special region"; and, finally, that the Red Army should become subject to the orders of the Military Council of the Nationalist government.

These arrangements took on a new urgency with the full-scale invasion of China by the Japanese beginning at Beijing on 7 July 1937. The Japanese forces thrust south and west and occupied most of north China by the end of the year. Another Japanese army attacked Shanghai from the sea in August and pushed on to Nanjing, the national capital, which they captured with incredible ferocity, massacring tens of thousands of civilians in December. During 1938 they advanced up the Yangzi Valley to Wuhan and beyond and finally occupied the great southern port city of Canton. The KMT government retreated into the Yangzi gorges, setting up a new capital in Chongqing. A People's Political Council was established in July 1938 in which thirty out of two hundred seats were allocated to the Communists. Communist military leaders, including Zhu De and Zhou Enlai, joined the Military Council.

The Red Army was reorganized as part of the United Front agreement. The main force, the Eighth Route Army in Shaanxi, was to be strictly limited to fifty thousand men, while a New Fourth Army was formed in central China to serve on the fluid front there. The New Fourth Army soon swelled far beyond the original limit of ten thousand men, recruiting new members as well as gathering up the remnants from the Long March and isolated bases. Since it was the only large regular Communist force in direct contact with both the KMT army and the Japanese it soon became a test of the willingness of both sides to co-operate.

The year 1940 was a very dark one for the KMT. The Japanese offensive had eased, partly to consolidate its gains, partly to regroup for further advances into South-East Asia. The morale of the KMT, shattered by the loss of half its territory, was further weakened by the defection of Wang Jingwei to head a puppet government in the Japanese-controlled areas. Mao took advantage of this situation by ordering an offensive in the north which brought much more territory under the control of the Eighth Route Army and hence the CCP.

It was becoming clear that the war against the Japanese was providing new opportunities for the CCP that might never have arisen otherwise. The restrictions on the size of the Red Army did not affect irregular guerrilla forces, which were to grow to half a million by 1945. Extensive areas throughout China came under effective control of the Communists, with the exception of the larger towns and railways, which the Japanese held. To hundreds of millions of Chinese, the CCP became the focus of national resistance.

During 1942 and 1943 the war in China remained static; meanwhile, internal faction fighting, inflation, and incompetence sapped the efficiency of the Nationalist armies and government. This was demonstrated dramatically in 1944 when a renewed Japanese offensive, aimed mainly at the airfields being used by the United States Air Force for raids on Japanese possessions and ultimately the Japanese islands, pushed aside the Chinese armies. Honan, already shattered by drought and famine, fell, as did Changsha, Guilin and Liuzhou. The United States reassessed its China-based strategy and opted for a thrust through the Pacific to Japan. Jiang Jie-shi's victory over his critics, like General Stilwell, who had been replaced for urging reforms too vigorously, was to prove extremely costly.

When the Pacific War ended, the situation in China was much more favourable to Mao's CCP than it had been at its beginning. Yet the advantage still appeared to lie with the Nationalists, and Mao himself confessed that at the time he did not foresee success in less than five years. The KMT was the government of a China that had won the war, however slight the Nationalist contribution to the victory. Jiang Jie-shi was one of the Big Four at the Cairo Conference, and even the USSR gave him government recognition and financial support. His military forces outnumbered those of Mao by perhaps four to one. He could rely on financial support and military supplies from the United States, now unquestionably the strongest world power with the atomic bomb added to its industrial might.

On what did Mao Zedong rest his confidence in eventual victory? In August 1946, in an interview with the American journalist Anna Louise Strong, Mao commented on his prospects when faced by a United States–backed KMT: "The atom bomb is a paper tiger which the US reactionaries use to scare people. It looks terrible but in fact it isn't. Of course, the atom bomb is a weapon of mass slaughter, but the outcome of a war is decided by the people." Perhaps there was a little whistling in the dark here — certainly the Chinese leaders developed atomic weapons as quickly as possible — but as Mao went on to say, a popular mass movement must triumph in the long run over an unpopular regime.

We have only millet plus rifles to rely on, but history will finally prove that our millet plus rifles is more powerful than Jiang Jie-shi's aeroplanes plus tanks. Although the Chinese people still face many difficulties and will long suffer hardship from the joint attacks of U.S. imperialism and the Chinese reactionaries, the day will come when these reactionaries are defeated and we are victorious. The reason is simply this: the reactionaries represent reaction, we represent progress.

The Civil War

Neither Mao Zedong nor Jiang Ji-shi had any illusions that the end of World War II would not mark the beginning of a renewed struggle for China. The United States attempted to play a mediating role, urging a coalition government for China, and the CCP and the KMT sought to gain diplomatic advantages, but both realized that war was the only outcome.

As the Japanese armies surrendered, there was a scramble to occupy the surrendered territories. In north China, the Red Army nearly doubled its area of control in late 1945, while Lin Biao's forces occupied most of Manchuria. They gained large supplies of Japanese arms as the Russian troops withdrew but little of the industrial equipment from the Japanese factories and mines, which the Russians dismantled and sent back to the USSR. Nor did they control the large cities, which the KMT occupied in a massive airlift in American planes. They were content to surround the cities, cutting off ground supply lines, and to await the eventual surrender of the besieged garrisons. What seemed at the time a bold coup by Jiang Jie-shi was to lead to the loss of his crack regiments with little fighting.

The United States had been attempting to negotiate a settlement since late 1944 when President Roosevelt sent a close adviser, Patrick Hurley, as his special envoy. Hurley, who seems never to have appreciated the real situation in China, eventually blamed the Communists for the breakdown of negotiations, but his own naivety and duplicity were at least as much the cause. The most he achieved was a face-to-face encounter between Jiang and Mao, who flew from Yan'an to Chongqing. This meeting, the first for twenty years, under American auspices, confirmed the fundamental and total incompatibility of the two major Chinese parties.

Mao was not averse to a coalition on his terms, because he realized that it would gain him valuable time and that its breakdown might be blamed on the KMT. He readily enough agreed to reduce his forces, since the CCP strength lay in militia and guerrilla units which would not be included in the agreement. He insisted, however, on recognition by the KMT of the Communist-controlled base areas as semi-independent units in a Chinese federation. Similarly, he accepted a two-to-one advantage of the KMT in the membership of the proposed council of the coalition government, since the remaining ten of the forty seats in that body would include some of the smaller parties favourable to the CCP, and he needed only fourteen votes to veto proposals (two-thirds being required for major decisions).

The conference broke down, Hurley was recalled, and General Marshall arrived in November 1945 to continue mediation. In mid-1946 a new United States ambassador, an old China hand, Leighton Stuart, was appointed. But by January 1947, when Marshall returned to the United States, America had largely wiped its hands of China. It granted massive aid and loans, but the American people were in no mood for remobilization so soon after the war, and concern was focused on Europe rather than Asia. When open fighting broke out again, it was once more a purely Chinese civil war.

The CCP victory that followed was a military one but one achieved with surprisingly little actual fighting. Whole armies surrendered without a shot, and an observer of the Communist entry into Beijing in January 1949 noted that most of the Red Army's equipment were the very tanks, trucks, and arms supplied by the United States to the KMT. The Nationalist regime collapsed from within, sapped by inept leadership, galloping inflation, brutality, and war weariness. The Communists promised a change, often vaguely and incorrectly understood, but a change that many Chinese saw to be inevitable, the "mandate of Heaven".

The course of the 1947–49 civil war is best seen as a three-phase struggle. The first in the spring and summer of 1947 saw the KMT armies advance into the Communist strongholds in the north, even capturing Yan'an itself in March 1947. As in Manchuria, however, the concentration on the cities proved fatal. The mobile Communist forces simply retreated, regrouped in the countryside, and broke the main road and rail lines of communication. Then in late 1947 and early 1948 the Red Army struck back in swift attacks into the north-east, central China, and the Huai Valley. It was at this time that the greatest battles were fought, especially for control of Loyang, Kaifeng, and

Xuzhou. Finally the cities in Manchuria and north China, including Mukden, Beijing, and Tianjin, were taken by direct attack. The spring campaign of 1949 was more a mopping-up operation than a battle. The Red Army crossed the Yangzi unopposed, took Nanjing, Canton, Sichuan, and eventually Hainan island, the last major area to fall in April 1950.

The KMT government withdrew to the island of Taiwan, to which Jiang Jie-shi, who had "retired" on 21 January 1949, leaving Vice-President Li Zongren to conduct the formal surrender, had transferred the treasury and the party and army organs still loyal to him. It was probably only the outbreak of the Korean War in June 1950, which brought the US Seventh Fleet into the Straits of Taiwan, that prevented the conquest of all the traditional territory of China by Mao Zedong's armies. On 10 October 1949 the People's Republic of China was formally proclaimed, with Mao Zedong as its chairman. An exhausted country was at peace at last.

Mao's China, 1950-66

Paradoxically, the accession of Mao to total power in 1949 marks the beginning of a period when Mao the man becomes more elusive than ever. We know much of his public acts, formal speeches, and authoritative writings, but what went on within the leaders' quarters in the old imperial palace just off Tianan Men Square remains mysterious and conjectural. Roxane Witke's interviews with Jiang Qing suggest deep tensions in which old rivalries and ideological differences plagued the inner-party group.

In Beijing itself Mao had to contend with the party apparatus controlled by the organizing genius of Liu Shaoqi. The Premier, Zhou Enlai, while always loyal to Mao and not a direct rival to Mao's authority like Liu, was responsible for governing a quarter of mankind and securing China a place in a troubled, changing world. Mao's inclination to confrontation and struggle and his anti-bureaucratic instincts proved a constant trial to his lieutenants, who had to bring order and efficiency to a war-ravaged society.

In the provinces, Mao had the further problem of the entrenched power of the military commanders who had set up the six administrative regions and military control commissions to administer the hand-over of power. Less evident as a threat at the time, but perhaps even more decisive for the future, was the control of the south central region and its capital Wuhan by Lin Biao's Fourth Field Army.

Mao made no secret of the long-term aim of socialism. China would build a powerful state apparatus which would eventually (although only when the time was ripe, not immediately) implement socialism through the nationalization of all private industry and the socialization of agriculture. "Our present policy", he said, "is to regulate capitalism, not to destroy it." Mao also proclaimed in the first years a massive modernization programme which he characteristically described as "a new

10,000 *li* long march". More pragmatically, the state planners devised the First Five-Year Plan, to begin in 1953, giving priority to heavy industry over consumer goods and agriculture.

To implement these development plans, as well as to secure China externally, it was essential to normalize relations with the Soviet Union. We have already seen that, until very late in the civil war, Stalin had maintained good relations with the KMT government; and Mao Zedong had never been a favourite of Moscow. Hence his first major task was to build bridges with the Russians.

In December 1949 Mao for the first time travelled outside China, going to Moscow to meet Stalin. It was not the cordial encounter that the rest of the world assumed it to be. It took Mao nine weeks before he gained grudging support from the Russians for China's economic development, and then in the form of small loans amounting to a mere US$60 million per year. Russia and China formed a mutual defence pact against Japan (which was hardly an immediate threat in 1949). In return, Russia exacted approval for her continued occupation of Port Arthur and Dairen, as well as recognition of the Mongolian People's Republic. It is a measure of Mao's statesmanship that Mao never allowed this experience to sour his admiration, at least in public, for Stalin, although we may also see in this incident the roots of the later Sino-Soviet dispute.

During the first year of the People's Republic, however, events forced China more firmly than she probably wished into the Soviet bloc. In June 1950 North Korean forces attacked across the border into the south and the Korean War began. China was caught by surprise; she had nothing to gain from the war when she seemed on the brink of a successful invasion of Taiwan and consequent recognition by the United States. Now she was dragged into support of her Communist allies in a traditionally Chinese sphere of influence. In October her forces entered North Korea and eventually engaged the US armies.

The Korean War was a setback for Mao not so much because of its stalemated outcome as because of its domestic consequences. China was forced to devote scanty resources to a military buildup; to accept Russian military aid and advice, and, more seriously, as the war developed into a technical slogging match, to professionalize her army along Russian lines. The people's army was in danger of becoming the people's master.

Internally, the gradualism of Mao's earlier policies yielded to a massive campaign of coercion against "counter-revolutionaries". During the so-called "Three Anti" and "Five Anti" campaigns of 1951-52, large numbers of people were investigated, imprisoned, and executed. The official figures (probably an underestimate) admit to a million or more arrested and several hundred thousand executed. When added to the victims of the land reform campaign, the total far exceeds that of the casualties of the civil war. Mao and the Chinese government have often blamed the excesses of this period on spontaneous reaction of the people against their oppressors and the climate created by the continuing KMT threat to the southern coastal regions and the war in Korea. While this is true, and Mao's speeches in 1950-51 emphasize due process and "not hitting out in all directions", such directives as the succinct one of 19 December 1950 — "Please make certain that you strike surely, accurately and relentlessly in suppressing the counter-revolutionaries" — surely contributed to the violence.

More characteristic of Mao's approach, however, was the emphasis on "thought reform", an extension and application to the whole nation of the methods of the rectification campaign of the early 1940s. Persuasion was to be through self-examination, confession, and group pressure rather than force. While more overt use of force, detention without trial, and labour camps certainly existed in Mao's China and is admitted by his successors, Mao the teacher preferred persuasion and conviction. It might be questioned, however, whether it is any less totalitarian to break the mind rather than the body.

One of the earliest measures of social reform introduced by the new government was one dear to Mao since his student days — changes to the marriage law. Choice of marriage partner was to be free; child marriage, polygamy, and concubinage were abolished. In China, as elsewhere, the equality of women proved much easier in legislation than in reality, but serious attempts were made to give women positions of authority at all levels of the government.

The thorniest problem facing Mao and the Communist authorities was of course land reform. The land revolution in Red-occupied territory during the anti-Japanese and civil wars had displaced landlords and rich peasants, often with violence. Experienced cadres urged that the same methods of struggle meetings and dispossession be applied nation-wide. At first Mao (or perhaps his advisers) resisted and pushed for a "rich peasant economy" analogous to the toleration of the national capitalists in industry. A stable agricultural economy was an essential underpinning for industrial development, and only the landlords were to be stripped of their land and punished. Co-operatives consisting of several households, pooling land, animals and machinery, were encouraged but not prescribed.

From mid-1955, collectivization was accelerated. Mao set a target for autumn 1956 of 1.3 million rural co-operatives, with full socialization to be achieved in three years. In his "On the Co-operative Transformation of Agriculture" (July 1955), he proclaimed his confidence in the socialist aspirations of the peasants. After five years of Communist government there had emerged a "high tide of social transformation in the countryside". And he dismissed his critics as "tottering along like a woman with bound feet . . . complaining all the time, 'You're going too fast, much too fast.' ".

Mao's supreme self-confidence in the triumph of his ideas was soon to reach its zenith in the "Hundred Flowers" campaign. The intellectuals had received little special treatment from the party in the first years of the People's Republic, and Mao had joined the "literary tsar", Zhou Yang, in the bitter attack on the dissident writer Hu Feng in 1955. However, 1956 was a very disturbed year for the international Communist movement, with Khrushchev's attacks on Stalin and disturbances in Eastern Europe. While some of the Chinese leaders reacted fearfully, Mao was convinced that China had nothing to fear from the open discussion and debate of problems within Chinese society and the CCP itself.

In an extraordinary statement in January 1957 Mao expressed his belief that "poisonous weeds" had only to be seen for them to be rejected for the "fragrant flowers" of socialist thought, and urged the publication of the *Collected Works of Chiang Kai-shek* so that people could see what a bad man he was. "It is correct to let a hundred flowers bloom and a hundred schools of thought contend," he said. "Truth develops in the struggle with falsehood. Beauty develops in comparison with and in struggle against ugliness. Good things and good men develop in comparison with and in struggle against bad men."

On 27 February 1957 Mao returned to this theme in what was to be his last important theoretical essay, "On the Correct Handling of Contradictions among the People". China was now united, and the struggle was now with an external enemy.

However, there would continue to be "non-antagonistic" co[ntra]dictions within the Chinese people itself. The resolution [of] these internal contradictions would be through peaceful means and by democratic methods. The intellectuals still required "remoulding" to replace bourgeois world views with a proletarian outlook. This remoulding would only be possible if "different forms and styles in art" and "different schools in science" were allowed to contend freely. Arbitrary and bureaucratic solutions would not convince people but force the struggle into violent and unproductive forms.

In response to Mao's invitation, criticisms began to be published in newspapers and journals and as "big-character posters" on walls and notice-boards. At first cautious and general, in mid-1957 they began to be more strident, to be directed against specific policies and against the leaders of the CCP. At this point (which, in the light of later events, may have been foreseen and intended by Mao) the party leaders closed ranks and initiated an "Anti-Rightist Movement" to suppress their critics. Mao, again foreshadowing his later tactics in similar circumstances, left Beijing for Shanghai, whose more radical party committee was more congenial to him. Soon he was directing the anti-rightist campaign against tendencies within the party itself and encouraging the relegation of party and state bureaucrats to engage in manual work in the countryside.

The First Five Year Plan was drawing to its close at the end of 1957, and despite its striking success of a 15 per cent annual growth rate in industry, Mao was unhappy with its Russian-style emphasis on the cities and heavy industries. He proposed an alternative policy, a "Great Leap Forward", which would reverse the priorities and simultaneously develop city and country. Decision-making was to be decentralized. It was the old guerrilla tactics applied to the economy — "walking on two legs", Mao called it. If China needed steel, let it be made in "backyard furnaces". If the peasants needed tractors, let them build them for themselves.

The mobilization of the people required for the Great Leap Forward demanded new forms of social organization. Perhaps spurred on by the growing tensions with the Soviet Union and a desire to demonstrate China's advanced socialism, the rural collectives were amalgamated in late 1958 into people's communes providing communal mess-halls, social services, and schools.

Then, spurred on by the "high tide" in the countryside, some cities began forming urban communes.

By the end of 1958, however, it was becoming evident that the optimistic forecasts of the Great Leap Forward were not being fulfilled. The harvest was bad, partly due to the shift of labour to the communal factories and workshops. Many of the goods produced were so poor in quality as to be unusable. At the same time the United States had increased its military aid to Taiwan and there was threat of an invasion.

When the Central Committee of the CCP met in Wuzhang in December 1958, Mao's opponents took the initiative. They stopped many of the innovations, restored central control of planning and accounting, and condemned the excesses of the Great Leap Forward. Mao's reply was to resign as Chairman of the republic — that is, head of the government — although he remained as head of the party, the more important position. It is probably not the case that Mao was literally forced out of office, but his resignation was a victory for Liu Shaozi, who succeeded him in the office of state Chairman. There is no doubt that Mao both resented his loss of control and blamed Liu for his reverses.

In foreign policy, too, 1957–58 saw Mao's policies under threat. In November 1957 Mao visited Moscow a second time for a conference of Communist Party representatives. There was no open breach between the Chinese and Russians, but when Mao remarked that "the East Wind prevails over the West Wind" he is more likely to have had eastern and western Communism in mind than to have included the USSR in his "East". Nevertheless, their differences led logically to Khrushchev's rapprochement with the United States and China's support of liberation movements in Asia and Africa. By July 1960 Soviet experts were withdrawn, causing much ill feeling. At the November 1960 Moscow World Conference of Communist Parties the split became open amid mutual charges of revisionism, and in the mid-1960s actual fighting occurred along the Russian-Chinese border. China and Russia had now become great-power rivals as well as presenting the major alternative models for communism.

By the end of his first decade of power, then, Mao Zedong's reputation was under a cloud. The Great Leap Forward had been a disaster, although not entirely as a result of Maoist policies. The year 1959 saw the first of three seasons of unusually bad conditions — floods, droughts, and consequent famine —

which strengthened the hand of Mao's enemies and diverted attention from the real achievements of the period. The Great Leap Forward had brought Mao's ideas as never before into the countryside, where the vast majority of China's people still lived, and had given the peasants a glimpse of a society in which the dominance of the cities might not always hold.

Mao himself was not to sink into impotence or anonymity. In July 1959 Peng Dehuai, Minister of Defence and the former commander in Korea, addressed a long "letter of opinion" to the Central Committee of the CCP soon after his return from a trip to Moscow. Peng attacked the Great Leap Forward and, by implication, Mao. Mao's reply was strong and immediate. At the party conference in Lushan he fought back, using language that was coarse and earthy and which appealed beyond the party to the people. He refused to take all responsibilty for the failure of the fifties and lashed out at his opponents. He admitted his mistakes but defended the experiment as a vast school in which "a population of several hundred million and several million cadres got an education".

The outcome of the Lushan meeting of August 1959 was the condemnation of Peng for "right opportunism" and anti-party activities, and the removal of Peng and his supporters from office. Lin Biao became Minister of Defence and Luo Ruiqing Chief of Staff of the army. But the result was more a stalemate than a decisive victory for Mao Zedong. It was probably as much due to Peng's alleged treasonous contacts with Khrushchev as to sympathy with Mao, and there was no reversal of economic policies. Mao had effectively been "kicked upstairs" with the status of Sage of the Revolution but no longer trusted to run the affairs of state. He now spent most of his time in the southern resort of Hangzhou and wrote several poems reflecting a mood of retirement and contemplation:

> Lost in my dreams, undisturbed,
> Of a hibiscus land in which the morning sun always shine.

But the dreams were not as peaceful as the poem implies, as events soon showed.

The Great Proletarian Cultural Revolution

There has been much speculation about when Mao Zedong decided on the counter-attack which became the Great Proletarian Cultural Revolution. In many respects it stemmed from removal of Peng Dehuai and his replacement in control of the army by Lin Biao. This made the PLA a potential power-base for the "Maoists" against Liu Shaoqi and the party apparatus. More immediately, though, the Tenth Plenum of the Central Committee in September 1962 marked Mao's return to a more active leadership role.

Mao is said on this occasion to have dropped hints of future action against revisionists within the party which passed unremarked only because his views were no longer taken as seriously as before. Another reason for the comparative lack of concern was that Mao's attention seemed diverted from the political to the cultural sphere. He expressed concern about the ghost, or remnants of feudal attitudes to be found in Peking opera and encouraged his wife, Jiang Qing, to organize a festival of Peking operas on contemporary themes in July 1964. But those who knew Mao's views on the relation between literature and the arts and politics should have been warned.

On 10 November 1965 a little-known writer, Yao Wenyuan, published an article in a Shanghai newspaper attacking the play "Hui Jui Dismissed from Office", first performed in 1961 and written by the historian and deputy mayor of Peking, Wu Han. It is certain that Yao was writing with the knowledge and probably prompting of Mao Zedong, who had been spending much time in Shanghai. It is also clear that Wu Han and his friends in the Peking establishment was the centre of the opposition to Mao within the CCP.

What may not be so clear is what a play had to do with the power struggle within the party leadership. It was not, however, mere coincidence. Wu Han was well known as a historian who during the Japanese occupation had "used the past to satirize the present". Now, in his play he had written about an upright Ming dynasty official who suppressed tyrannous local officials and returned land seized by them to the people only to be dismissed by the Emperor because of pressure from the officials' corrupt friends in high places. The question was: Who did the emperor stand for? There could be little doubt. Wu was a friend and bridge-partner of the party General Secretary, Deng Xiaoping. As deputy mayor he was close to Peng Zhen, the mayor of Peking and leading critic of the "Hundred Flowers" movement. He had collaborated with Deng Tuo, secretary of the Peking Party Committee, on a series of articles in the *People's Daily* called "Records of the Three Family Village" which contained many thinly veiled cracks about Mao and his policies.

The *People's Daily* took nearly three weeks to reprint the critical article, which suggests a resistance of the Peking group to Mao's new campaign. Then, as the debate developed, it published almost as many defences of Wu Han as attacks on him, until February 1966 when the balance began to change against him. By April it was clear that the attack on Wu was a stalking-horse for much larger prey.

On 18 April 1966 the term "Great Proletarian Cultural Revolution" first appeared in the Shanghai *Liberation Daily* (in an article not reprinted until 4 May in the *People's Daily*). An attempt to appropriate the Maoist initiative was the establishment of a Cultural Revolution Committee led by none other than Peng Zhen. But in a circular of the Central Committee of the CCP sent to all top party members on 16 May 1966 this committee was dissolved and a new Cultural Revolution Group created, directly under the Standing Committee of the Political Bureau, and headed by Chen Boda, Mao Zedong's secretary. This circular for the first time pointed to anti-party and anti-socialist tendencies within the party, even (pointedly) within the Central Committee.

Mao's role up until this point seems to have been essentially that of the guerrilla fighter working from within and in the minority. If the campaign was to succeed in its aim of deposing those in power — that is, a majority of the Central Committee who opposed him — it required new forces from outside. In a characteristically bold move he appealed directly to the young and the disaffected, running the risk of destroying the party as a result. On 25 May the first "big-character poster" went up at Beijing University attacking the president and the vice-secretary of the party. Within a few weeks all schools and universities were closed down for the duration of the Cultural Revolution, many not to reopen for up to seven years. The youth of China took to the streets, and open warfare between opposing groups began.

If there was any doubt regarding the direct role of Chairman Mao, it was resolved on 16 July when Mao made a much-publicized swim in the Yangzi. According to the reports, the seventy-two-year-old leader swam with thousands of youngsters about fourteen kilometres downstream in a little over an hour. Although this was with the current, it was about four times the Olympic record for the distance! Whatever actually happened, the incident had great symbolic importance. Mao was not only alive but in his full powers and at the head of the revolutionary youth of China.

This same message was proclaimed more formally at the beginning of August when the Central Committee issued the sixteen points programme of the Great Proletarian Cultural Revolution. It discounted the moderate line officially pursued by the party up until now and specifically attacked "those party persons in power taking the capitalist road". Although it urged persuasion rather than violence (perhaps a last desperate throw by Liu Shaoqi and the "moderates") Mao's own poster issued at the time, "Bombard the Headquarters", was in a very different spirit.

Mao and his defenders have often denied the old man's responsibility for the violence of the year that followed. Although he was not, as it were, the director, he was at least the stage manager. He encouraged the "long marches" of "Red Guards" from all over China to Beijing and received them in mass rallies in Tianan Men Square. He and the Cultural Revolution Group, which included his wife, Jiang Qing; Kang Sheng, an old comrade; and the Shanghai activists Yao Wenyuan and Zhang Chunqiao, constantly intervened in support of the radicals in the struggles that erupted in most major Chinese cities. Only in Shanghai did Mao personally apply the brakes after the proclamation of a commune in January 1967. In the most serious incident, a full-scale civil war in Wuhan in July 1967, Mao, through his envoy Zhou Enlai, supported the Red Guards against the army.

Nevertheless, by late 1967 even Mao seems to have had enough. Liu Shaoqi was by now thoroughly discredited as the top party person taking the capitalist road. His formal deposition in October 1968 was an afterthought. Zhou Enlai was dismayed at the damage done to China's foreign relations and image abroad. He called in the PLA to defend the Foreign Ministry and was furious when the Red Guards sacked the British Chancellery in Beijing. It had proved much easier to destroy the old than to create a new order to replace it. What perilous semblance of public order remained was due to the army alone and could not be prolonged indefinitely.

The Red Guards were dealt with summarily by dispatching them *en masse* to the countryside. New revolutionary committees were created at all levels to govern until the party could be rectified and restored. Cadres (i.e., bureaucrats, party officials, managers of all levels) were sent to May 7 Cadre Schools devoted to political re-education and purification by labour. Workers' Propaganda Teams and PLA-based Mao Zedong Thought Teams were sent into educational institutions to advance proletarian consciousness.

By the Ninth Party Congress in April 1969 some normality was restored, and the party organs began to function again. Perhaps the most significant move at the congress was the new party constitution which unprecedentedly named Lin Biao as Mao's successor. We do not know Mao's views on this apart from a few guarded criticisms expressed to Edgar Snow in an interview in 1970 about Lin's role in the excessive personally cult. Yet there is no reason to believe that Mao Zedong had abandoned his view that the party must always control the gun, and Lin represented above all the gun, the PLA, which had largely by default emerged from the Cultural Revolution as the arbiter of Chinese politicals. Mao's ambiguous final remarks to Snow that he was a lonely monk walking the world under a leaky umbrella suggests that once more he felt himself pushed aside.

Mao Zedong's last years, until his death on 9 September 1976, were marked by failing health and a struggle for succession. A procession of Western leaders, including US President Richard Nixon in February 1972, found him mentally alert but physically frail. Whatever the truth of the frequent stories about his incognito midnight visits to read the posters during the Cultural Revolution, he was now totally dependent upon his entourage, a dying emperor surrounding by fawning courtiers. Yet the old unpredictability and guile still surfaced dramatically.

The most remarkable incident, and one still largely a mystery to the Chinese themselves as much as to outsiders, is the Lin Biao Affair. In late 1971 Lin Biao suddenly disappeared from view, but it was only in May 1972 that a version of his downfall was made public outside inner party circles. The story was that Lin had led a coup on 12 September 1971, involving the attempted assassination of Chairman Mao. Warned in time, Mao had been whisked off the train destined to be blown up, and Lin and his co-plotters, mostly high-ranking service officers, had attempted to flee by air to Russia but crashed near the Mongolian border.

We will not rehearse here the various improbabilities of the official account. It strains credulity ridiculously to believe that the tough professional soldier was secretly writing Confucian tags in his diary, or that the conspirators would have compiled an incriminating and detailed outline for an uprising, praising Japanese *bushido* values, linking themselves with the Soviet Union, and so on. But Lin was dead and Mao, now without a named successor, alive.

Mao's open break with Lin appears to date from the Lushan meeting of the Central Committee in August-September 1970 when Lin and his ally Chen Boda lost their bid to prevent the calling of the National People's Congress. Mao then began systematically criticizing the Lin group and replacing PLA commanders loyal to the Vice-Chairman. As the net closed in, Lin Biao may well have been forced into a rash act, some allege at the instigation of his wife and son. His former leftist allies of the Cultural Revolution, including Jiang Qing, had abandoned him; his fall, whatever the details, was inevitable.

The post-Mao mythology presents the power struggle of 1971-76 as a battle between Zhou Enlai and his bureaucratic group on the one hand and the Gang of Four on the other. The Gang of Four, comprising Jiang Qing, Yao Wenyuan, Zhang Chunqiao, and Wang Hungwen, are alleged to have plotted against Zhou, even against Mao himself. Mao is said to have become estranged from his wife and warned his intimates against her.

All this is far too neat. The Gang of Four continued to be promoted, presumably with Mao's approval, up until 1975, when all were appointed vice-premiers. Yet when Zhou Enlai died in January 1976 it was Mao's fellow-provincial, the little-known Hua Guofeng who was appointed as Premier, and Wang Hungwen found the resurrected Deng Xiaoping as his fellow

Vice-Chairman of the party. Mao's rare statements (or rather those attributed to him) from the last years are enigmatic and have been given far too much weight. His actions speak much more clearly. As with many a Chinese emperor before him, it proved too difficult to name a successor, and Mao "went to meet Marx" as he once put it, leaving the children to settle it themselves.

Epilogue

While the biography of Mao Zedong ends in 1976, Mao's influence continues to mark China, even — or perhaps especially — in those areas where he has been found wanting by the new leaders. Most of them are still of the Mao generation, men whose ideas and policies were formed by daily contact and conflict with him.

There is a protean, many-sided quality to the leaders of great modern revolutions that resists stereotyping. In the twentieth century, Lenin, Sun Yatsen, Kemel Ataturk, Sukarno have all possessed to a high degree the power to inspire wildly divergent currents of thought and action. Mao too had that power to move people in directions he neither foresaw nor perhaps approved.

When Huo Guofeng published, amid much acclaim, in 1977 the fifth volume of the *Selected Works of Mao Zedong*, consisting of the writings of the early and mid 1950s, he was not repudiating the revolutionary Mao of Yan'an and the Cultural Revolution but pointing to Mao the planner and consolidator. Perhaps his successors will find the young Mao or the later Mao of more relevance to China's problems. But I do not believe they or we will be able to ignore him.

In a poem written in 1961 after seeing the opera "The Monkey King", Mao Zedong, obviously comparing himself to the mischievous, combative, irrepressible Monkey, wrote what might be his own epitaph:

> The Monkey King brandished his mighty staff,
> And the heavens were cleared of dust for thousands of miles.
> Today let us proclaim the Monkey Sage,
> As once more the miasma closes in on us.

Further Reading

Bianco, L. *Origins of the Chinese Revolution, 1915-1949*. Stanford, Cal.: Stanford University Press, 1971.
Ch'en, J. *Mao and the Chinese Revolution*. London: Oxford University Press, 1965.
Mao Zedong. *Selected Works*. 5 vols. Beijing: Foreign Language Press, 1963-77.
_____. *Poems*. Beijing: Foreign Languages Press, 1976.
_____. *The Political Thought of Mao Tse-tung*. Edited by Stuart Schram. Harmondsworth, Middx.: Penguin, 1969.
_____. *Mao Tse-tung Unrehearsed*. Edited by Stuart Schram. Harmondsworth, Middx.: Penguin, 1974.
Schram, S. *Mao Tse-tung*, Penguin, 1966.
Selden, M. *The Yenan Way in Revolutionary China*. Cambridge, Mass.: Harvard University Press, 1971.
Smart, N. *Mao*. London: Fontana, 1974.
Snow, E. *Red Star Over China*. London: Gollancz, 1937 (rev. ed., Penguin, 1972).
_____. *China's Long Revolution*. Harmondsworth, Middx.: Penguin, 1974.
Terrill, R. *Mao: A Biography*. New York: Harper and Row, 1980.
Wilson, D. *Mao: The People's Emperor*. London: Futura, 1980.
Witke, R. *Comrade Chiang Ch'ing*. London: Weidenfeld and Nicolson, 1977.

Index

Anyuan, miners strike, 8

Beijing (Peking), 5, 6, 23, 29, 35, 42, 43
Borodin, Comintern representative, 13
Braun, Otto, 18, 19

Changsha, 2, 3, 4, 5; autumn harvest rising, 13, 14
Chen Boda, Mao's secretary, 43, 46
Chen Duxiu, secretary general, CCP, 4, 5, 7, 8, 12
Chen Yi, 14
Chinese Communist Party (CCP), formation of, 8; relations with USSR, 36, 38
Chongqing, capital of Sichuan, 20, 29
Communes, 39, 40
Cultural Revolution, 25, 42-45

Dadu (Tatu) River, 20
Deng Xi'aopeng, 43, 46

Gang of Four, 46
Great Leap Forward Campaign, 39-40, 41
Guiyang, capital of Guizhou, 20
Guomindang (KMT), 9, 10, 11, 14-15, 16, 18, 34

Hailufeng, 11
Hanzhou, 41
He Zizhen, Mao's second wife, 17, 24
Ho Lung, 19, 21
Hu Feng, writer, 38
Hua Guofeng, 46, 48
Hundred Flowers campaign, 38, 39

Japanese, 18, 26, 28-30
Jiang Jie-shi (Chiang Kai Shek), 9, 12, 16, 18, 20, 22, 28, 30, 34
Jiang Qing, Mao's third wife, 24, 35, 42, 44, 46
Jinggangshan, 14

Korean War, 34, 36

Land reform, 37, 38
Li Dazhao, 5, 6
Li Lisan, 8, 10, 15
Lin Biao, 14, 32, 35, 41, 42, 45, 46
Lui Shaoqi, 8, 35, 40, 44
Long March, 18-21
Lu Xun Academy, 23
Luding, 20
Luo Ruiqing, 41

Manchuria, 28
Mao Zedong: in power, 35-47; rural revolution, 11-17; War, 28-34; the Yan'an Years, 22-27; Young Revolutionary, 6-10; Youth, 1-5. See also Long March
Mao Xemin, Mao's brother, 12
Marshall, US general, 33
May Fourth Movement, 7
Mongolia, 36, 46
Moscow, 36, 40, 41. See also Stalin

Nanchang August rising, 13
Nanjing, national capital, 29
New Peoples Study Society, 4, 7
Nixon, president of USA, 45
Northern Expedition, 11

Peng Dehuai, Fifth army leader, Defence Minister, 14, 15, 41, 42

Peng Pai, early agrarian revolutionary, 11
Peng Zhen, 43
Peoples Republic of China, proclaimed 10 October 1949, 34

Red Army (Peoples Liberation Army), 22-23, 29, 32, 45
Red Guards, 44, 45
Ruijin, early Chinese Soviet capital, 15

Seeckt, General Hans von, 17
Shaanxi, 18, 21, 28
Shanghai, 8, 10, 12, 42, 44
Shaushan, Mao's birthplace, 1, 10
Snow, Edgar, 1, 2, 3, 6, 24, 45
Stalin, 13, 36, 38
Strong, Anna Louise, 30
Sun Yatsen, 9, 12

United Front, KMT/CCP of 1923-27, 9, 12, 13; Second United Front, 28
USSR, relations with, 36, 40. *See also* Moscow

Wang Jingwei, 11, 13, 29

Wang Ming, 16, 26
Whampoa, military academy, 9
Wuhan, 3, 15, 29, 35, 44; CCP's 5th Congress at, 12; Central committee at, 40
Wu Han, major of Beijing, 42, 43

Xi'om, 22, 28

Yan'an (Yenan), 21, 22-26, 33, 48
Yang Changji, Mao's teacher, 3, 6
Yang Hucheng, and the Xi'an incident, 28
Yang Kaihui, Mao's first wife, 6, 7, 13
Yuan Shikai, 3, 4
Yunan, 20

Zang Guotao, 9, 20, 21, 26
Zang Jingyao, military governor of Henan, 7
Zhang Xueliang, Manchurian leader, 28
Zhou Enlai, Mao's comrade, 6, 9, 13, 16, 18, 28, 29, 35, 44, 45, 46
Zhou Yang, 38
Zhu De, 13, 14, 15, 16, 18, 20, 21, 29